# FLAGS
## of the WORLD
# STICKER ATLAS

# AFGHANISTAN

| | |
|---|---|
| **Population:** | 16,592,000 |
| **Capital:** | Kabul |
| **Languages:** | Pushtu, Dari, Persian, Faarse, Furkic |
| **Geography:** | Area: 251,773 Sq. Miles (about the size of Texas) |
| **Religions:** | Sunni Muslim, Shiite Muslim |
| **National Day:** | April 27 |

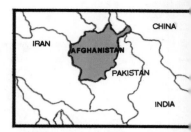

# ALBANIA

| | |
|---|---|
| **Population:** | 3,268,000 |
| **Capital:** | Tiranë |
| **Languages:** | Albanian (Tosk is official dialect) |
| **Geography:** | Area: 11,100 Sq. Miles (slightly larger than Maryland) |
| **Religions:** | Atheist, Muslim |
| **National Day:** | November 28 |

# ALGERIA

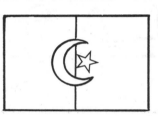

| | |
|---|---|
| **Population:** | 25,714,000 |
| **Capital:** | Algiers |
| **Geography:** | Area: 918,497 Sq. Miles (more than three times the size of Texas) |
| **Religion:** | Sunni Muslim |
| **National Days:** | July 3, November 1 |

# ANDORRA

| | |
|---|---|
| **Population:** | 56,000 |
| **Capital:** | Andorra la Vella |
| **Languages:** | Catalan (official), Spanish, French |
| **Geography:** | Area: 185 Sq. Miles (half the size of New York City) |
| **Religion:** | Roman Catholic |
| **National Day:** | September 8 |

# ANGOLA

| | |
|---|---|
| **Population:** | 8,960,000 |
| **Capital:** | Luanda |
| **Languages:** | Portugese, Umbunder, Kimbundu, Lunda, Kikongo |
| **Geography:** | Area: 481,353 Sq. Miles (larger than Texas and California combined) |
| **Religions:** | Roman Catholic, Protestant |
| **National Days:** | February 4, November 11, December 10 |

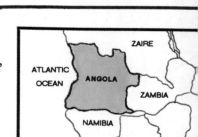

# ARGENTINA

| | |
|---|---|
| **Population:** | 32,291,000 |
| **Capital:** | Buenos Aires |
| **Language:** | Spanish, Italian, English, German, French |
| **Geography:** | Area: 1,065,189 Sq. Miles (four times the size of Texas) |
| **Religion:** | Roman Catholic |
| **National Days:** | May 25, July 9 |

# ARMENIA

| | |
|---|---|
| **Population:** | 3,293,000 |
| **Capital:** | Yerevan |
| **Language:** | Armenian |
| **Geography:** | Area: 11,580 Sq. Miles |

# AUSTRALIA

| | |
|---|---|
| **Population:** | 17,233,000 |
| **Capital:** | Canberra |
| **Languages:** | English, aboriginal languages |
| **Geography:** | Area: 2,966,200 Sq. Miles (almost as large as the continental United States) |
| **Religions:** | Anglican, Protestant, Roman Catholic |
| **National Day:** | January 26 |

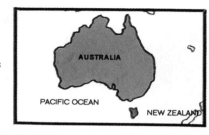

# AUSTRIA

| | |
|---|---|
| **Population:** | 7,595,000 |
| **Capital:** | Vienna |
| **Language:** | German |
| **Geography:** | Area: 32,374 Sq. Miles (slightly smaller than Maine) |
| **Religion:** | Roman Catholic |
| **National Day:** | October 26 |

# AZERBAIJAN

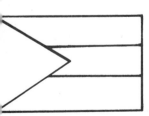

| | |
|---|---|
| **Population:** | 7,131,000 |
| **Capital:** | Baku |
| **Language:** | Azeri |
| **Geography:** | Area: 33,590 Sq. Miles |

# BAHAMAS

| | |
|---|---|
| **Population:** | 251,000 |
| **Capital:** | Nassau |
| **Language:** | English & Creole |
| **Geography:** | 5,380 Sq. Miles (about the size of Connecticut) |
| **Religions:** | Baptist, Anglican, Roman Catholic |
| **National Day:** | July 10 |

# BAHRAIN

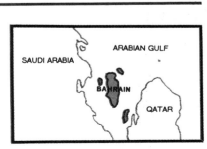

| | |
|---|---|
| **Population:** | 512,000 |
| **Capital:** | Manama |
| **Languages:** | Arabic (official), Farsi, Urdu |
| **Geography:** | Area: 258 Sq. Miles (smaller than New York City) |
| **Religions:** | Sunni Muslim, Shiite Muslim |
| **National Day:** | December 16 |

# BANGLADESH

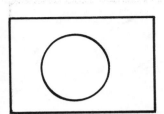

| | |
|---|---|
| **Population:** | 117,976,000 |
| **Capital:** | Dhaka |
| **Languages:** | Bengali (official), English |
| **Geography:** | Area: 55,598 Sq. Miles (slightly smaller than Wisconsin) |
| **Religions:** | Muslim, Hindu |
| **National Days:** | February 21, March 26, December 16 |

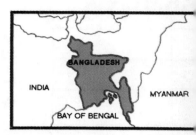

# BARBADOS

| | |
|---|---|
| **Population:** | 260,000 |
| **Capital:** | Bridgetown |
| **Language:** | English |
| **Geography:** | Area: 166 Sq. Miles |
| **Religions:** | Anglican, Methodist, Roman Catholic and Pentecostal |
| **National Day:** | November 30 |

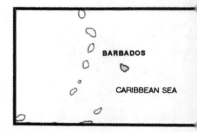

# BELARUS

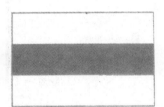

| | |
|---|---|
| **Population:** | 10,259,000 |
| **Capital:** | Minsk |
| **Language:** | Belarussian |
| **Geography:** | Area: 80,310 Sq. Miles |

# BELGIUM

| | |
|---|---|
| **Population:** | 9,895,000 |
| **Captial:** | Brussels |
| **Language:** | Flemish, French, German |
| **Geography:** | Area: 11,799 Sq. Miles (slightly larger than Maryland) |
| **Religion:** | Roman Catholic |
| **National Day:** | July 21 |

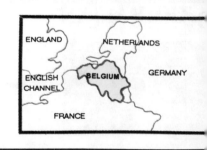

# BELIZE

| | |
|---|---|
| **Population:** | 204,000 |
| **Capital:** | Belmopan |
| **Languages:** | English, Spanish, Creole |
| **Geography:** | Area: 8,867 Sq. Miles |
| **Religions:** | Roman Catholic, Protestant |
| **National Days:** | September 10, September 21 |

# BENIN

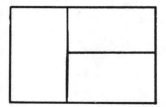

| | |
|---|---|
| **Population:** | 4,840,000 |
| **Capital:** | Porto-Novo |
| **Languages:** | French, local dialects, Fon, Yoruba, Sonba |
| **Geography:** | Area: 43,483 Sq. Miles |
| **Religions:** | Mainly Animist with Christian and Muslim minorities |
| **National Day:** | November 30 |

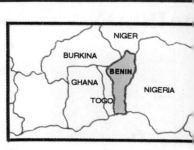

# BERMUDA

| | |
|---|---|
| **Population:** | 58,800 |
| **Capital:** | Hamilton |
| **Language:** | English |
| **Geography:** | 20.6 Sq. Miles |

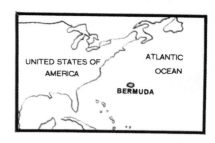

# BHUTAN

| | |
|---|---|
| **Population:** | 1,566,000 |
| **Capital:** | Thimphu |
| **Languages:** | Dzongkha, Nepalese dialects |
| **Geography:** | Area: 18,147 Sq. Miles |
| **Religions:** | Buddist, Hindu |
| **National Day:** | December 17 |

# BOLIVIA

| | |
|---|---|
| **Population:** | 7,157,000 |
| **Capital:** | Sucre (legal capital and seat of judiciary: La Paz seat of government) |
| **Languages:** | Spanish, Quechua, Aymara |
| **Geography:** | Area: 424,165 Sq. Miles |
| **Religion:** | Roman Catholic |
| **National Day:** | August 6 |

# BOSNIA - HERZEGOVINA

| | |
|---|---|
| **Capital:** | Sarajevo |

# BOTSWANA

| | |
|---|---|
| **Population:** | 1,218,000 |
| **Capital:** | Gaborone |
| **Languages:** | English, Tswana |
| **Geography:** | Area: 231,804 Sq. Miles (slightly smaller than Texas) |
| **Religions:** | indigenous beliefs, Christian |
| **National Day** | September 30 |

# BRAZIL

| | |
|---|---|
| **Population:** | 153,771,000 |
| **Capital:** | Brasilia |
| **Languages:** | Portuguese, English, Spanish, French |
| **Geography:** | Area: 3,286,470 Sq. Miles (larger than the contiguous 48 United States) |
| **Religion:** | Roman Catholic |
| **National Day:** | September 9 |

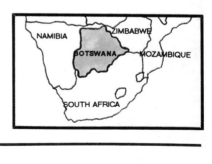

# BRUNEI

| | |
|---|---|
| **Population:** | 398,000 |
| **Capital:** | Bandar Seri Begawan |
| **Languages:** | Malay, English, Chinese |
| **Geography:** | Area: 2,226 Sq. Miles (smaller than Delaware) |
| **Religions:** | Muslim, Buddhist, Christian |
| **National Days:** | January 1, February 23, June 15 |

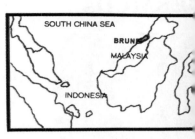

# BULGARIA

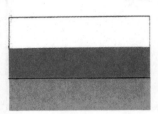

| | |
|---|---|
| **Population:** | 8,978,000 |
| **Capital:** | Sofia |
| **Languages:** | Bulgarian, Turkish, Greek |
| **Geography:** | Area: 44,365 Sq. Miles (about the size of Ohio) |
| **Religions:** | Government promotes atheism; background of people is Orthodox |
| **National Day:** | September 9 |

# BURKINA

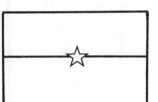

| | |
|---|---|
| **Population:** | 8,941,000 |
| **Capital:** | Ouagadougou |
| **Languages:** | French, Sudaric tribal languages |
| **Geography:** | Area: 105,869 Sq. Miles (the size of Colorado) |
| **Religions:** | Animist, Muslim, Christian |
| **National Day:** | August 4 |

# BURUNDI

| | |
|---|---|
| **Population:** | 5,831,000 |
| **Capital:** | Bujumbura |
| **Languages:** | French, Rundi |
| **Geography:** | Area: 10,760 Sq. Miles |
| **Religions:** | Christian, traditional African |
| **National Day:** | July 1 |

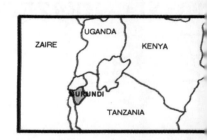

# CAMBODIA

| | |
|---|---|
| **Population:** | 7,350,000 |
| **Capital:** | Phnom Penh |
| **Languages:** | Khmer, French |
| **Geography:** | Area: 69,898 Sq. Miles (the size of Missouri) |
| **Religion:** | Theravada Buddhism |

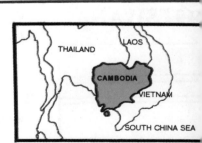

# CAMEROON

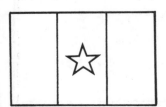

| | |
|---|---|
| **Population:** | 11,109,000 |
| **Capital:** | Yaounde |
| **Languages:** | French, English, Fulani, Bantu |
| **Geography:** | Area: 185,568 Sq. Miles (somewhat larger than California) |
| **Religions:** | Animist, Muslin, Christian |
| **National Day:** | May 20 |

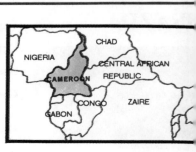

# CANADA

| | |
|---|---|
| **Population:** | 26,527,000 |
| **Capital:** | Ottawa |
| **Languages:** | English, French |
| **Geography:** | Area: 3,558,096 Sq. Miles (second largest country in land size) |
| **Religions:** | Roman Catholic, Protestant |
| **National Day:** | July 1 |

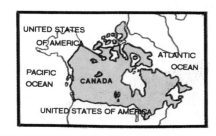

# CENTRAL AFRICAN REPUBLIC

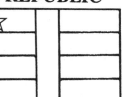

| | |
|---|---|
| **Population:** | 2,879,000 |
| **Capital:** | Bangui |
| **Languages:** | French, Sango |
| **Geography:** | Area: 240,534 Sq. Miles (slightly smaller than Texas) |
| **Religions:** | Protestant, Roman Catholic, traditional |
| **National Day:** | December 1 |

# CHAD

| | |
|---|---|
| **Population:** | 5,240,000 |
| **Capital:** | N'Djamena |
| **Languages:** | French, Arabic |
| **Geography:** | Area: 495,755 Sq. Miles (four-fifths the size of Alaska) |
| **Religions:** | Muslin, Animist, Christian |
| **National Day:** | July 7 |

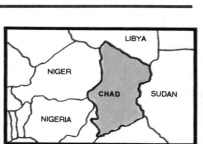

# CHILE

| | |
|---|---|
| **Population:** | 13,000,000 |
| **Capital:** | Santiago |
| **Languages:** | Spanish, Aruacanian |
| **Geography:** | Area: 292,257 Sq. Miles (larger than Texas) |
| **Religions:** | Roman Catholic, Protestant |
| **National Day:** | September 18 |

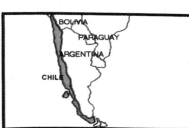

# CHINA

| | |
|---|---|
| **Population:** | 1,130,065,000 |
| **Capital:** | Beijing |
| **Languages:** | Mandarin Chinese, Yue, Wu Minbei, Minnan, Xiang, Gan |
| **Geography:** | Area: 3,705,390 Sq. Miles (slightly larger than the conterminous U.S. |
| **Religions:** | Atheist, Confucianist, Buddhist, Taoist |
| **National Day:** | October 1 |

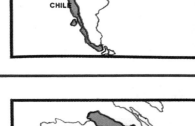

# COLOMBIA

| | |
|---|---|
| **Population:** | 33,777,000 |
| **Capital:** | Bogata |
| **Language:** | Spanish |
| **Geography:** | Area: 439,735 Sq. Miles (about the size of Texas, and New Mexico combined) |
| **Religion:** | Roman Catholic |
| **National Day:** | July 20 |

# COMOROS

| | |
|---|---|
| **Population:** | 459,000 |
| **Capital:** | Moroni |
| **Languages:** | Arabic, French, Comoran, Shaafi Islam, Malagasy |
| **Geography:** | Area: 838 Sq. Miles (half the size of Delaware) |
| **Religions:** | Sunni Muslim, Roman Catholic |
| **National Day** | November 12 |

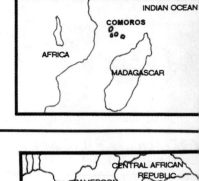

# CONGO

| | |
|---|---|
| **Population:** | 2,305,000 |
| **Capital:** | Brazzaville |
| **Languages:** | French, Monokutuba, Lingaia |
| **Geography:** | Area: 132,046 Sq. Miles (slightly smaller than Montana) |
| **Religions:** | Christian, Animist, Muslin |
| **National Day:** | August 15 |

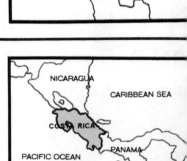

# COSTA RICA

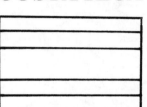

| | |
|---|---|
| **Population:** | 3,032,000 |
| **Capital:** | San Jose |
| **Language:** | Spanish |
| **Geography:** | Area: 19,575 Sq. Miles (smaller than West Virginia) |
| **Religion:** | Roman Catholic |
| **National Day:** | September 15 |

# CÔTE D'IVOIRE
(FORMALLY IVORY COAST)

| | |
|---|---|
| **Population:** | 12,070,000 |
| **Capital:** | Abidjan |
| **Languages:** | French, tribal languages |
| **Geography:** | Area: 124,503 Sq. Miles (slightly larger than New Mexico) |
| **Religions:** | Muslin, Christan |
| **National Day:** | December 7 |

# CROATIA

| | |
|---|---|
| **Capital:** | Zagreb |

# CUBA

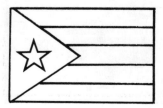

| | |
|---|---|
| **Population:** | 10,582,000 |
| **Capital:** | Havana |
| **Language:** | Spanish |
| **Geography:** | Area: 44,218 Sq. Miles (nearly as large as Pennsylvania) |
| **Religion:** | Roman Catholic, Pentecostal, Baptist |
| **National Days:** | January 1, July 26, October 10 |

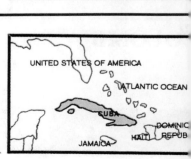

# YPRUS

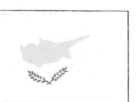

| | |
|---|---|
| **Population:** | 708,000 |
| **Capital:** | Nicosia |
| **Languages:** | Greek, Turkish, English |
| **Geography:** | Area: 3,572 Sq. Miles (smaller than Connecticut |
| **Religions:** | Orthodox, Muslin |
| **National Day:** | October 1 |

# ZECHOSLOVAKIA

| | |
|---|---|
| **Population:** | 15,695,000 |
| **Capital:** | Prague |
| **Languages:** | Czech, Slovak, Hungarian |
| **Geography:** | Area: 49,365 Sq. Miles (the size of New York) |
| **Religion:** | Roman Catholic, Protestant, Orthodox |
| **National Day:** | May 9 |

# ENMARK

| | |
|---|---|
| **Population:** | 5,134,000 |
| **Capital:** | Copenhagen |
| **Language:** | Danish & German |
| **Geography:** | Area: 16,633 Sq. Miles ( about the size of Massachusetts and New Hampshire combined) |
| **Religion:** | Evangelical Luthern |
| **National Days:** | April 16, June 5 |

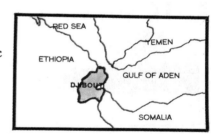

# JIBOUTI

| | |
|---|---|
| **Population:** | 470,000 |
| **Capital:** | Djibouti |
| **Languages:** | French, Arabic, Somali, Saho-Afar, Arabic |
| **Geography:** | Area: 8,950 Sq. Miles (about the size of New Hampshire) |
| **Religion:** | Sunni Muslin |
| **National Day:** | June 27 |

# OMINICAN REPUBLIC

| | |
|---|---|
| **Population:** | 7,253,000 |
| **Capital:** | Santo Domingo |
| **Language:** | Spanish |
| **Geography:** | Area: 18,816 Sq. Miles (the size of Vermont and New Hampshire combined) |
| **Religion:** | Roman Catholic |
| **National Day:** | February 27 |

# CUADOR

| | |
|---|---|
| **Population:** | 10,506,000 |
| **Capital:** | Quito |
| **Languages:** | Spanish, Quechuan, Jivaroan |
| **Geography:** | Area: 109,483 Sq. Miles (the size of Colorado) |
| **Religion:** | Roman Catholic |
| **National Day:** | August 18 |

# EGYPT

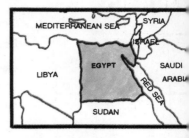

| | |
|---|---|
| **Population:** | 54,139,000 |
| **Capital:** | Cairo |
| **Languages:** | Arabic, English |
| **Geography:** | Area: 386,650 Sq. Miles (about the size of Texas, Oklahoma, and Arkansas combined) |
| **Religion:** | Sunni Muslim |
| **National Days:** | July 23, October 6 |

# EL SALVADOR

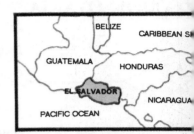

| | |
|---|---|
| **Population:** | 5,221,000 |
| **Capital:** | San Salvador |
| **Languages:** | Spanish, Nahuati |
| **Geography:** | Area: 8,260 Sq. Miles (the size of Massachusetts) |
| **Religion:** | Roman Catholic |

# EQUATORIAL GUINEA

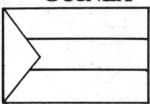

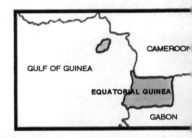

| | |
|---|---|
| **Population:** | 384,000 |
| **Capital:** | Malabo |
| **Languages:** | Spanish, Fang, Bubi, English |
| **Geography:** | Area: 10,832 Sq. Miles (the size of Maryland) |
| **Religion:** | Roman Catholic |
| **National Day:** | October 12 |

# ESTONIA

| | |
|---|---|
| **Population:** | 1,602,000 |
| **Capital:** | Tallinn |
| **Languages:** | Estonian, Russian |
| **Geography:** | Area: 17,412 Sq. Miles |
| **Religion:** | Lutheran |

# ETHIOPIA

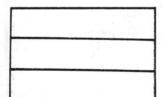

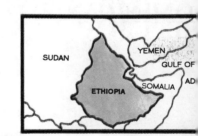

| | |
|---|---|
| **Population:** | 53,191,000 |
| **Capital:** | Addis Ababa |
| **Languages:** | Amharic, Tigre, Galla, Arabic |
| **Geography:** | Area: 471,776 Sq. Miles (four-fifths the size of Alaska) |
| **Religions:** | Orthodox Christian, Muslin |
| **National Day:** | September 12 |

# FIJI

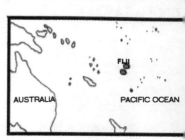

| | |
|---|---|
| **Population:** | 772,000 |
| **Capital:** | Suva |
| **Languages:** | English, Fijian, Hindustani |
| **Geography:** | Area: 7,056 Sq. Miles (the size of Massachusetts) |
| **Religions:** | Christian, Hindu, Muslin |
| **National Day:** | October 10 |

## FINLAND

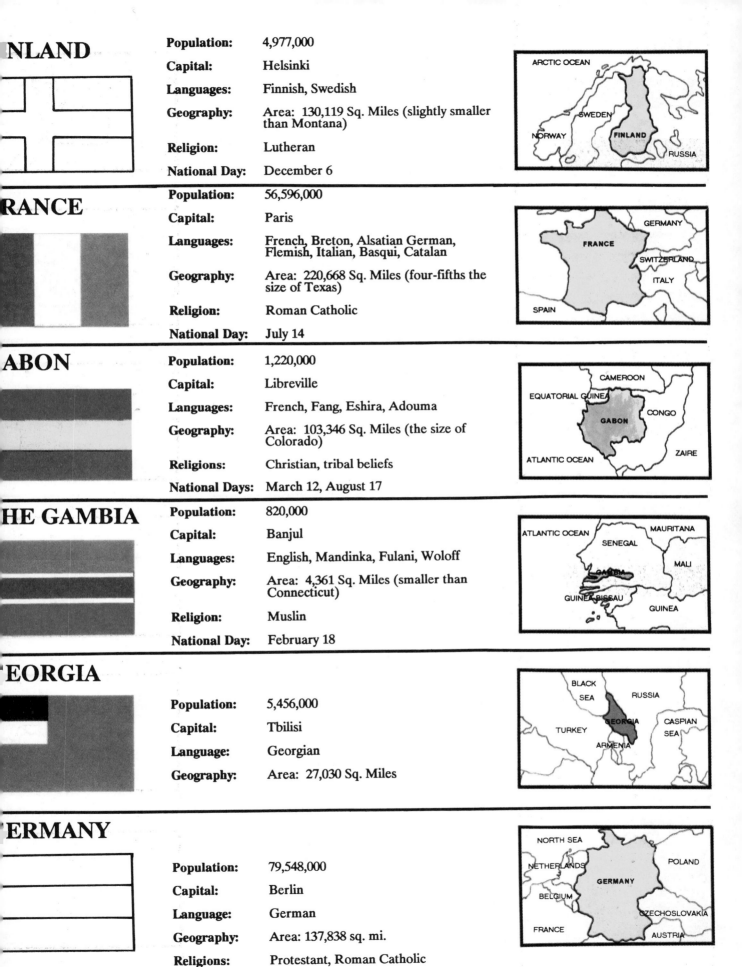

| | |
|---|---|
| **Population:** | 4,977,000 |
| **Capital:** | Helsinki |
| **Languages:** | Finnish, Swedish |
| **Geography:** | Area: 130,119 Sq. Miles (slightly smaller than Montana) |
| **Religion:** | Lutheran |
| **National Day:** | December 6 |

## FRANCE

| | |
|---|---|
| **Population:** | 56,596,000 |
| **Capital:** | Paris |
| **Languages:** | French, Breton, Alsatian German, Flemish, Italian, Basqui, Catalan |
| **Geography:** | Area: 220,668 Sq. Miles (four-fifths the size of Texas) |
| **Religion:** | Roman Catholic |
| **National Day:** | July 14 |

## GABON

| | |
|---|---|
| **Population:** | 1,220,000 |
| **Capital:** | Libreville |
| **Languages:** | French, Fang, Eshira, Adouma |
| **Geography:** | Area: 103,346 Sq. Miles (the size of Colorado) |
| **Religions:** | Christian, tribal beliefs |
| **National Days:** | March 12, August 17 |

## THE GAMBIA

| | |
|---|---|
| **Population:** | 820,000 |
| **Capital:** | Banjul |
| **Languages:** | English, Mandinka, Fulani, Woloff |
| **Geography:** | Area: 4,361 Sq. Miles (smaller than Connecticut) |
| **Religion:** | Muslin |
| **National Day:** | February 18 |

## GEORGIA

| | |
|---|---|
| **Population:** | 5,456,000 |
| **Capital:** | Tbilisi |
| **Language:** | Georgian |
| **Geography:** | Area: 27,030 Sq. Miles |

## GERMANY

| | |
|---|---|
| **Population:** | 79,548,000 |
| **Capital:** | Berlin |
| **Language:** | German |
| **Geography:** | Area: 137,838 sq. mi. |
| **Religions:** | Protestant, Roman Catholic |

# GHANA

| | |
|---|---|
| **Population:** | 15,310,000 |
| **Capital:** | Accra |
| **Languages:** | Akan, Ewe, Ga, English |
| **Geography:** | Area: 92,098 Sq. Miles (slightly smaller than Oregon) |
| **Religions:** | Christian, Muslin, traditional beliefs |
| **National Days:** | March 6, July 2 |

# GREECE

| | |
|---|---|
| **Population:** | 10,066,000 |
| **Capital:** | Athens |
| **Language:** | Greek |
| **Geography:** | Area: 51,146 Sq. Miles (the size of Alabama) |
| **Religion:** | Greek Orthodox |
| **National Day:** | March 25 |

# GREENLAND

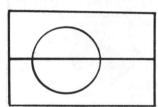

| | |
|---|---|
| **Population:** | 57,000 |
| **Capital:** | Nuuk (Godthab) |
| **Geography:** | Area: 840,000 Sq. Miles |

# GUATEMALA

| | |
|---|---|
| **Population:** | 9,340,000 |
| **Capital:** | Guatemala City |
| **Languages:** | Spanish, Indian dialects |
| **Geography:** | Area: 42,042 Sq. Miles (the size of Tennessee) |
| **Religion:** | Roman Catholic |
| **National Day:** | September 15 |

# GUINEA

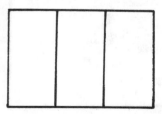

| | |
|---|---|
| **Population:** | 7,269,000 |
| **Capital:** | Conakry |
| **Languages:** | Fulani, Malinke, French |
| **Geography:** | Area: 94,964 Sq. Miles (slightly smaller than Oregon) |
| **Religions:** | Muslim, Christian |
| **National Day:** | October 2 |

# GUINEA - BISSAU

| | |
|---|---|
| **Population:** | 1,023,000 |
| **Capital:** | Bissau |
| **Languages:** | Portuguese, Criolo, tribal languages |
| **Geography:** | Area: 13,948 Sq. Miles (about the size of Connecticut) |
| **Religions:** | Traditional, Muslim, Christian |
| **National Day:** | September 10 |

# GUYANA

| | |
|---|---|
| **Population:** | 812,000 |
| **Capital:** | Georgetown |
| **Languages:** | English, Amerindian dialects |
| **Geography:** | Area: 83,000 Sq. Miles (the size of Idaho) |
| **Religions:** | Christian, Hindu, Muslin |
| **National Day:** | February 23 |

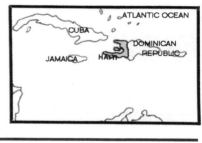

# HAITI

| | |
|---|---|
| **Population:** | 6,286,000 |
| **Capital:** | Port-au-Prince |
| **Languages:** | French, Creole |
| **Geography:** | Area: 10,714 Sq. Miles (the size of Maryland) |
| **Religions:** | Roman Catholic, Protestants, (Voodoo widely practiced) |
| **National Day:** | January 1 |

# HONDURAS

| | |
|---|---|
| **Population:** | 5,261,000 |
| **Capital:** | Tegucigalpa |
| **Languages:** | Spanish, aboriginal dialects |
| **Geography:** | Area: 43,277 Sq. Miles (slightly larger than Tennessee) |
| **Religion:** | Roman Catholic |
| **National Day:** | September 15 |

# HUNGARY

| | |
|---|---|
| **Population:** | 10,620,000 |
| **Capital:** | Budapest |
| **Language:** | Hungarian (Magyar) |
| **Geography:** | Area: 35,919 Sq. Miles (slightly smaller than Indiana) |
| **Religions:** | Roman Catholic, Protestant |
| **National Day:** | April 4 |

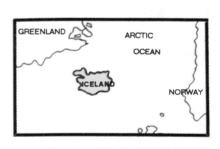

# ICELAND

| | |
|---|---|
| **Population:** | 251,000 |
| **Capital:** | Reykjavik |
| **Language:** | Icelandic (islenska) |
| **Geography:** | Area: 39,769 Sq. Miles (the size of Virginia) |
| **Religion:** | Evangelical Lutheran |
| **National Day:** | June 17 |

# INDIA

| | |
|---|---|
| **Population:** | 866,352,000 |
| **Capital:** | New Delhi |
| **Languages:** | Hindi, English, and 15 Indian languages |
| **Geography:** | Area: 1,266,595 Sq. Miles (one-third the size of the United States) |
| **Religions:** | Hindu, Muslim, Christian, Sikh |
| **National Days:** | January 26, August 15 |

# INDONESIA

| | |
|---|---|
| **Population:** | 193,560,000 |
| **Capital:** | Jakarta |
| **Languages:** | Bahasa Indonesian, Javanese, other Austronesian languages |
| **Geography:** | Area: 735,268 Sq. Miles |
| **Religion:** | Muslin |
| **National Days:** | August 17, December 27 |

# IRAN

| | |
|---|---|
| **Population:** | 59,051,000 |
| **Capital:** | Tehran |
| **Languages:** | Farsi, Turkish, Kurdish, Arabic, English, French |
| **Geography:** | Area: 636,293 Sq. Miles (slightly larger than Alaska) |
| **Religion:** | Shiite Muslim |
| **National Days:** | February 11, April 1 |

# IRAQ

| | |
|---|---|
| **Population:** | 18,782,000 |
| **Capital:** | Baghdad |
| **Languages:** | Arabic, Kurdish |
| **Geography:** | Area: 167,924 Sq. Miles (larger than California) |
| **Religions:** | Shiite Muslim, Sunni Muslim, Christian |
| **National Days:** | July 14, July 17 |

# IRELAND

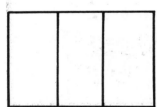

| | |
|---|---|
| **Population:** | 3,557,000 |
| **Capital:** | Dublin |
| **Languages:** | English, Irish |
| **Geography:** | Area: 27,137 Sq. Miles (slightly larger than West Virginia) |
| **Religions:** | Roman Catholic, Anglican |
| **National Day:** | March 17 |

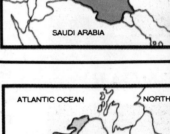

# ISRAEL

| | |
|---|---|
| **Population:** | 4,477,000 |
| **Capital:** | Jerusalem |
| **Languages:** | Hebrew, Arabic, Yiddish |
| **Geography:** | Area: 7,847 Sq. Miles (about the size of New Jersey) |
| **Religions:** | Jewish, Muslim |
| **National Day:** | May 15 |

# ITALY

| | |
|---|---|
| **Population:** | 57,657,000 |
| **Capital:** | Rome |
| **Language:** | Italian |
| **Geography:** | Area: 116,303 Sq. Miles (about the size of Florida and Georgia combined) |
| **Religion:** | Roman Catholic |
| **National Day:** | First Sunday in June |

# JAMAICA

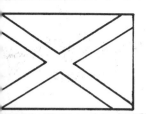

| | |
|---|---|
| **Population:** | 2,513,000 |
| **Capital:** | Kingston |
| **Languages:** | English, Jamaican Creole |
| **Geography:** | Area: 4,232 Sq. Miles (slightly smaller than Connecticut) |
| **Religion:** | Protestant |
| **National Day:** | First Monday in August |

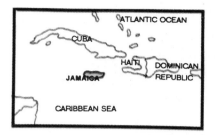

# JAPAN

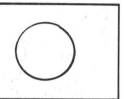

| | |
|---|---|
| **Population:** | 123,778,000 |
| **Capital:** | Tokyo |
| **Language:** | Japanese |
| **Geography:** | Area: 145,856 Sq. Miles (slightly smaller than California) |
| **Religions:** | Buddhist, Shintoist |
| **National Days:** | May 3, December 23 |

# JORDAN

| | |
|---|---|
| **Population:** | 3,412,000 |
| **Capital:** | Amman |
| **Languages:** | Arabic |
| **Geography:** | Area: 37,737 Sq. Miles (slightly larger than Indiana) |
| **Religions:** | Sunni Muslin, Christian |
| **National Day:** | May 25 |

# KAZAKHSTAN

| | |
|---|---|
| **Population:** | 16,691,000 |
| **Capital:** | Alma-Ata |
| **Language:** | Russian |
| **Geography:** | Area: 1,049,000 Sq. Miles |

# KENYA

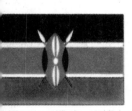

| | |
|---|---|
| **Population:** | 25,393,000 |
| **Capital:** | Nairobi |
| **Languages:** | Swahili, English, Kiswahili, Kikuyu |
| **Geography:** | Area: 224,960 Sq. Miles (slightly smaller than Texas) |
| **Religions:** | Protestant, Roman Catholic, Muslim |
| **National Days:** | June 1, October 20, December 12 |

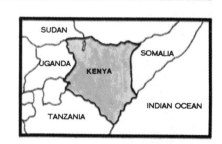

# NORTH KOREA

| | |
|---|---|
| **Population:** | 23,059,000 |
| **Capital:** | Pyongyang |
| **Language:** | Korean |
| **Geography:** | Area: 46,540 Sq. Miles (slightly smaller than Mississippi) |
| **Religions:** | Buddhist, Confucianist |
| **National Day:** | September 8 |

# POLITICAL MAP OF THE WORLD

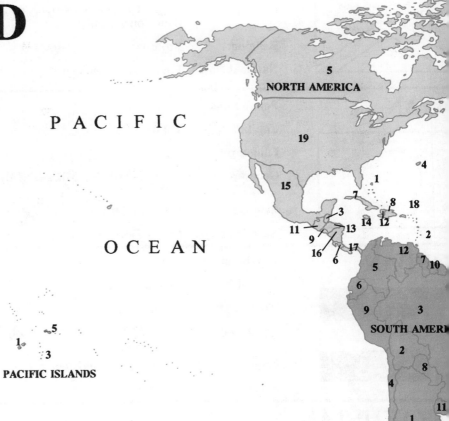

PACIFIC

OCEAN

NORTH AMERICA

5

19

15

4

1

7

3

8 18

11 14 12

9 13

16 17

6

2

12

5

7 10

6

3

9

SOUTH AMERI

2

8

4

11

1

5

3

PACIFIC ISLANDS

1

## AFRICA

1. ALGERIA
2. ANGOLA
3. BENIN
4. BOTSWANA
5. BURKINA
6. BURUNDI
7. CAMEROON
8. CENTRAL AFRICAN REPUBLIC
9. CHAD
10. COMOROS
11. CONGO
12. COTE D'IVOIRE
13. DJIBOUTI
14. EGYPT
15. EQUATORIAL GUINEA
16. ETHIOPIA
17. GABON
18. GAMBIA
19. GHANA
20. GUINEA
21. GUINEA-BISSAU
22. KENYA
23. LESOTHO
24. LIBERIA
25. LIBYA
26. MADAGASCAR
27. MALAWI
28. MALI
29. MAURITANIA
30. MAURITIUS
31. MOROCCO
32. MOZAMBIQUE
33. NAMIBIA
34. NIGER
35. NIGERIA
36. RWANDA
37. SENEGAL
38. SEYCHELLES
39. SIERRA LEONE
40. SOMALIA
41. SOUTH AFRICA
42. SUDAN
43. SWAZILAND
44. TANZANIA
45. TOGO
46. TUNISIA
47. UGANDA
48. ZAIRE
49. ZAMBIA
50. ZIMBABWE

## ASIA

1. AFGHANISTAN
2. ARMENIA
3. AZERBAIJAN
4. BAHRAIN
5. BANGLADESH
6. BHUTAN
7. BRUNEI
8. CAMBODIA
9. CHINA
10. CYPRUS
11. GEORGIA
12. INDIA
13. INDONESIA
14. IRAN
15. IRAQ
16. ISRAEL
17. JAPAN
18. JORDAN
19. KAZAKHSTAN
20. NORTH KOREA
21. SOUTH KOREA
22. KUWAIT
23. KYRGHYZSTAN
24. LAOS
25. LEBANON
26. MALAYSIA
27. MONGOLIA
28. MYANMAR
29. NEPAL
30. OMAN

31. PAKISTAN
32. PHILIPPINES
33. QATAR
34. RUSSIA (ASIAN)
35. SAUDI ARABIA
36. SINGAPORE
37. SRI LANKA
38. SYRIA
39. TAJIKISTAN
40. TAIWAN
41. THAILAND
42. TURKEY
43. TURKMENISTAN
44. UNITED ARAB EMIRATES
45. UZBEKISTAN
46. VIETNAM
47. YEMEN

## AUSTRALIA

1. AUSTRALIA
2. NEW ZEALAND
3. PAPUA NEW GUINEA

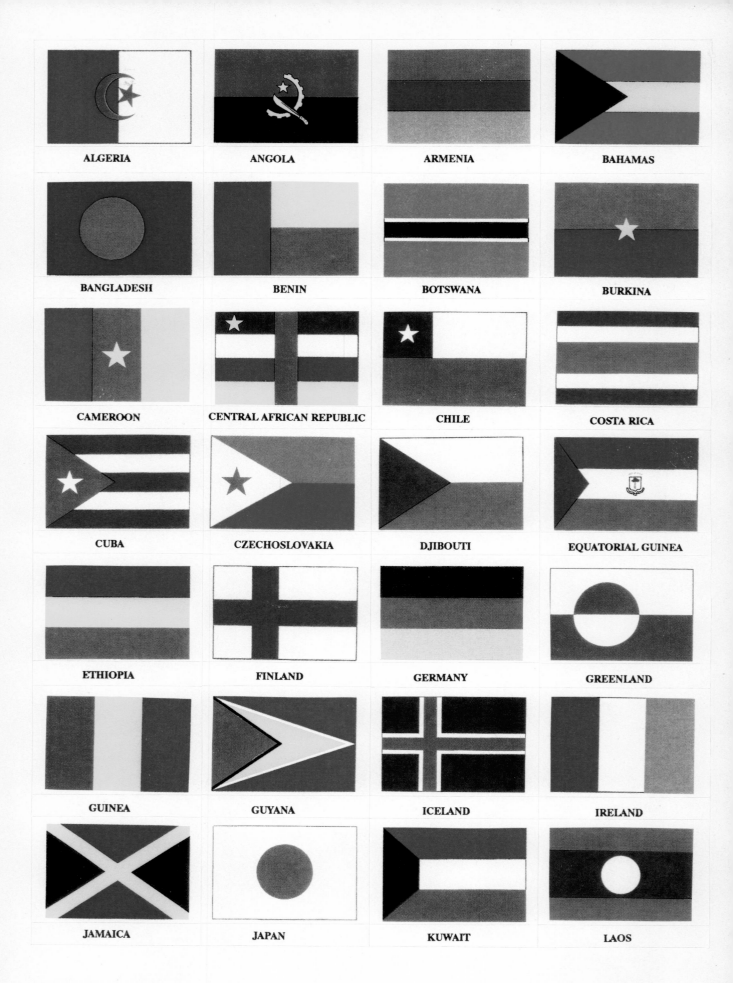

ALGERIA     ANGOLA     ARMENIA     BAHAMAS

BANGLADESH     BENIN     BOTSWANA     BURKINA

CAMEROON     CENTRAL AFRICAN REPUBLIC     CHILE     COSTA RICA

CUBA     CZECHOSLOVAKIA     DJIBOUTI     EQUATORIAL GUINEA

ETHIOPIA     FINLAND     GERMANY     GREENLAND

GUINEA     GUYANA     ICELAND     IRELAND

JAMAICA     JAPAN     KUWAIT     LAOS

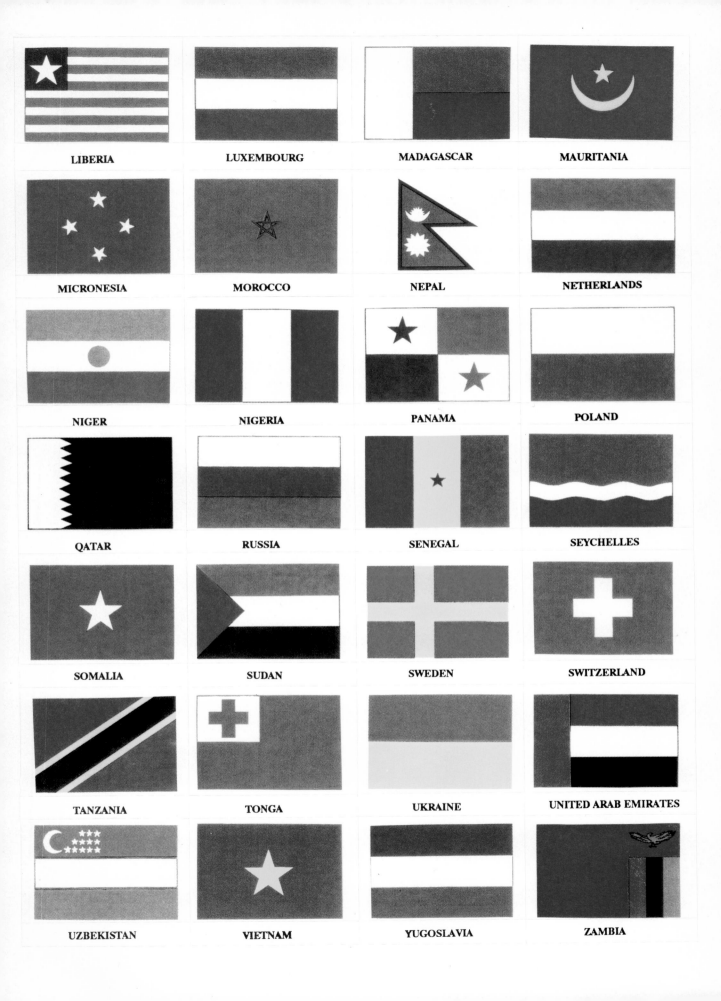

LIBERIA

LUXEMBOURG

MADAGASCAR

MAURITANIA

MICRONESIA

MOROCCO

NEPAL

NETHERLANDS

NIGER

NIGERIA

PANAMA

POLAND

QATAR

RUSSIA

SENEGAL

SEYCHELLES

SOMALIA

SUDAN

SWEDEN

SWITZERLAND

TANZANIA

TONGA

UKRAINE

UNITED ARAB EMIRATES

UZBEKISTAN

VIETNAM

YUGOSLAVIA

ZAMBIA

**EUROPE**

1. ALBANIA
2. ANDORRA
3. AUSTRIA
4. BELARUS
5. BELGIUM
6. BOSNIA-HERZEGOVINA
7. BULGARIA
8. CROATIA
9. CZECHOSLOVAKIA
10. DENMARK
11. ESTONIA
12. FINLAND
13. FRANCE
14. GERMANY
15. GREECE
16. HUNGARY
17. ICELAND
18. IRELAND
19. ITALY
20. LATVIA
21. LIECHTENSTEIN
22. LITHUANIA
23. LUXEMBOURG
24. MALTA
25. MOLDOVA
26. NETHERLANDS
27. NORWAY
28. POLAND
29. PORTUGAL
30. ROMANIA
31. RUSSIA (EUROPEAN)

32. SLOVENIA
33. SPAIN
34. SWEDEN
35. SWITZERLAND
36. UNITED KINGDOM
37. UKRAINE
38. VATICAN CITY
39. YUGOSLAVIA


**NORTH AMERICA**

1. BAHAMAS
2. BARBADOS
3. BELIZE
4. BERMUDA
5. CANADA
6. COSTA RICA
7. CUBA
8. DOMINICAN REPUBLIC
9. EL SALVADOR
10. GREENLAND
11. GUATEMALA
12. HAITI
13. HONDURAS
14. JAMAICA
15. MEXICO
16. NICARAGUA
17. PANAMA
18. PUERTO RICO
19. UNITED STATES

**SOUTH AMERICA**

1. ARGENTINA
2. BOLIVIA
3. BRAZIL
4. CHILE
5. COLOMBIA
6. ECUADOR
7. GUYANA
8. PARAGUAY
9. PERU
10. SURINAME
11. URUGUAY
12. VENEZUELA


**PACIFIC ISLANDS**

1. FIJI
2. MICRONESIA
3. TONGA
4. VANUATU
5. WESTERN SAMOA

# SOUTH KOREA

| | |
|---|---|
| **Population:** | 43,919,000 |
| **Capital:** | Seoul |
| **Language:** | Korean |
| **Geography:** | Area: 38,025 Sq. Miles (slightly larger than Indiana) |
| **Religions:** | Buddhist, Confucianist, Christian |
| **National Day:** | August 15 |

# KUWAIT

| | |
|---|---|
| **Population:** | 2,080,000 |
| **Capital:** | Kuwait |
| **Language:** | Arabic |
| **Geography:** | Area: 6,880 Sq. Miles (slightly smaller than New Jersey) |
| **Religion:** | Muslin |
| **National Day:** | February 25 |

# KYRGHYZSTAN

| | |
|---|---|
| **Population:** | 4,367,000 |
| **Capital:** | Bishkek |
| **Geography:** | Area: 76,830 Sq. Miles |

# LAOS

| | |
|---|---|
| **Population:** | 4,024,000 |
| **Capital:** | Vientiane |
| **Languages:** | Lao, French, Thai |
| **Geography:** | Area: 91,428 Sq. Miles (slightly larger than Utah) |
| **Religions:** | Buddhist, tribal |
| **National Day:** | December 2 |

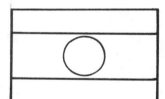

# LATVIA

| | |
|---|---|
| **Population:** | 2,738,000 |
| **Capital:** | Riga |
| **Languages:** | Latvian, Russian |
| **Geography:** | Area: 24,595 Sq. Miles |
| **Religions:** | Roman Catholic, Lutheran |

# LEBANON

| | |
|---|---|
| **Population:** | 3,500,000 |
| **Capital:** | Beirut |
| **Languages:** | Arabic, French, Armenian |
| **Geography:** | Area: 4,015 Sq. Miles (smaller than Connecticut) |
| **Religions:** | Muslim, Christian |
| **National Day:** | November 22 |

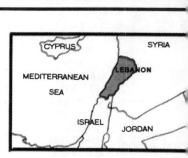

# ESOTHO

| | |
|---|---|
| **Population:** | 1,757,000 |
| **Capital:** | Maseru |
| **Languages:** | Sesotho, English |
| **Geography:** | Area: 11,716 Sq. Miles (slightly larger than Maryland) |
| **Religions:** | Roman Catholic, Protestant |
| **National Day:** | October 4 |

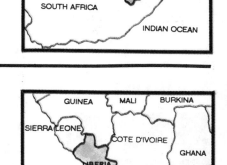

# IBERIA

| | |
|---|---|
| **Population:** | 2,644,000 |
| **Capital:** | Monrovia |
| **Languages:** | English, tribal dialects |
| **Geography:** | Area: 38,250 Sq. Miles (slightly smaller than Pennsylvania) |
| **Religions:** | Muslim, Christian, Animist |
| **National Day:** | July 26 |

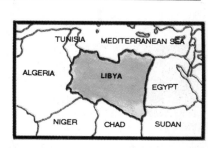

# IBYA

| | |
|---|---|
| **Population:** | 4,280,000 |
| **Capital:** | Tripoli |
| **Language:** | Arabic |
| **Geography:** | Area: 679,359 Sq. Miles (larger than Alaska) |
| **Religion:** | Sunni Muslim |
| **National Day:** | September 1 |

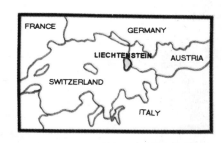

# IECHTENSTEIN

| | |
|---|---|
| **Population:** | 30,000 |
| **Capital:** | Vaduz |
| **Languages:** | German, Alemannic dialect |
| **Geography:** | Area: 62 Sq. Miles (the size of Washington D.C.) |
| **Religions:** | Roman Catholic, Protestant |
| **National Day:** | August 16 |

# ITHUANIA

| | |
|---|---|
| **Population:** | 3,760,000 |
| **Capital:** | Vilnius |
| **Languages:** | Lithuanian, Russian, Polish |
| **Geography:** | Area: 25,174 Sq. Miles |
| **Religion:** | Roman Catholic |

# UXEMBOURG

| | |
|---|---|
| **Population:** | 369,500 |
| **Capital:** | Luxembourg |
| **Languages:** | Luxembourgish, German, French |
| **Geography:** | Area: 998 Sq. Miles (smaller than Rhode Island) |
| **Religion:** | Roman Catholic |
| **National Day:** | June 23 |

# MADAGASCAR

| | |
|---|---|
| **Population:** | 11,802,000 |
| **Capital:** | Antananarivo |
| **Languages:** | French, Malagasy |
| **Geography:** | Area: 226,657 Sq. Miles (slightly smaller than Texas) |
| **Religions:** | Animist, Christian, Muslim |
| **National Day:** | June 26 |

# MALAWI

| | |
|---|---|
| **Population:** | 8,432,000 |
| **Capital:** | Lilongwe |
| **Languages:** | Chichewa, English |
| **Geography:** | Area: 45,747 Sq. Miles (the size of Pennsylvania) |
| **Religions:** | Christian, Muslim, Protestant |
| **National Day:** | July 6 |

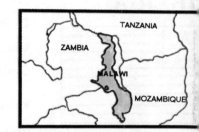

# MALAYSIA

| | |
|---|---|
| **Population:** | 17,915,000 |
| **Capital:** | Kuala Lamper |
| **Languages:** | Malay, Chinese, English |
| **Geography:** | Area: 129,251 Sq. Miles (slightly larger than New Mexico) |
| **Religions:** | Muslim, Hindu, Buddhist, Confucianist, Taoist, local religions |
| **National Day:** | August 31 |

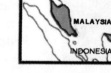

# MALI

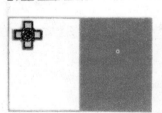

| | |
|---|---|
| **Population:** | 9,182,000 |
| **Capital:** | Bamako |
| **Languages:** | Bambara, Senufo |
| **Geography:** | Area: 478,764 Sq. Miles (about the size of Texas and California combined) |
| **Religion:** | Muslim |
| **National Day:** | September 22 |

# MALTA

| | |
|---|---|
| **Population:** | 373,000 |
| **Capital:** | Valletta |
| **Languages:** | Maltese, English |
| **Geography:** | Area: 122 Sq. Miles (twice the size of Washington D.C.) |
| **Religion:** | Roman Catholic |
| **National Day:** | March 31 |

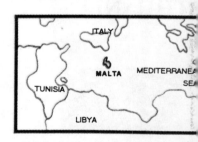

# MAURITANIA

| | |
|---|---|
| **Population:** | 2,038,000 |
| **Capital:** | Nouakchott |
| **Languages:** | French, Hassanya Arabic, Toucouleur |
| **Geography:** | Area: 397,954 Sq. Miles (the size of Texas and California combined) |
| **Religion:** | Muslim |
| **National Day:** | November 28 |

# MAURITIUS

| | |
|---|---|
| **Population:** | 1,141,900 |
| **Capital:** | Port Louis |
| **Languages:** | English, French, Creole, Bhujpuri |
| **Geography:** | Area: 790 Sq. Miles (about the size of Rhode Island) |
| **Religions:** | Hindu, Christian, Muslim |
| **National Day:** | March 12 |

# MEXICO

| | |
|---|---|
| **Population:** | 90,007,000 |
| **Capital:** | Mexico City |
| **Languages:** | Spanish, Indian languages, Ameridian |
| **Geography:** | Area: 761,604 Sq. Miles (three times the size of Texas) |
| **Religion:** | Roman Catholic |
| **National Day:** | September 16 |

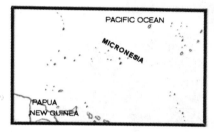

# MICRONESIA

| | |
|---|---|
| **Population:** | 108,000 |
| **Capital:** | Palikir |
| **Languages:** | Yapese, Ponapean, Trukese, Kosraean, Ulithian, Woleaian, Nukuoran, Kapingamarangi |
| **Geography:** | Area: 270 Sq. Miles |

# MOLDOVA

| | |
|---|---|
| **Population:** | 4,362,000 |
| **Capital:** | Chisinau |
| **Language:** | Romanian |
| **Geography:** | Area: 13,130 Sq. Miles |

# MONGOLIA

| | |
|---|---|
| **Population:** | 2,185,000 |
| **Capital:** | Ulan Bator |
| **Languages:** | Khalkha Mongolian, Ulaanbaatar, Russian, Chinese |
| **Geography:** | Area: 604,247 Sq. Miles (more than twice the size of Texas) |
| **Religion:** | Lama Buddhist |
| **National Day:** | July 11 |

# MOROCCO

| | |
|---|---|
| **Population:** | 26,249,000 |
| **Capital:** | Rabat |
| **Languages:** | Arabic, Berber, French |
| **Geography:** | Area: 172,413 Sq. Miles (larger than California) |
| **Religion:** | Sunni Muslim |
| **National Days:** | March 3, August 14 |

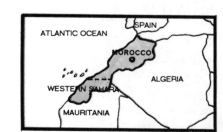

# MOZAMBIQUE

| | |
|---|---|
| **Population:** | 15,113,000 |
| **Capital:** | Maputo |
| **Languages:** | Portuguese, Swahili |
| **Geography:** | Area: 303,769 Sq. Miles (about the size of Texas) |
| **Religion:** | Traditional beliefs, Christian, Muslim |
| **National Day:** | June 25 |

# MYANMAR
## (FORMALLY BURMA)

| | |
|---|---|
| **Population:** | 41,279,000 |
| **Capital:** | Yangon |
| **Languages:** | Burmese, Kaven, Shan |
| **Geography:** | Area: 261,789 Sq. Miles (nearly as large as Texas) |
| **Religions:** | Buddist, Muslim, Christian |

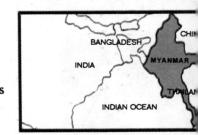

# NAMIBIA

| | |
|---|---|
| **Population:** | 1,904,000 |
| **Capital:** | Windhoek |
| **Languages:** | English, Afrikaans, Ovambo |
| **Geography:** | Area: 317,818 Sq. Miles (slightly more than half the size of Alaska) |
| **Religion:** | Lutheran, Roman Catholic |

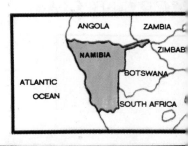

# NEPAL

| | |
|---|---|
| **Population:** | 19,158,000 |
| **Capital:** | Kathmandu |
| **Languages:** | Nepali, Bihari |
| **Geography:** | Area: 56,136 Sq. Miles (the size of North Carolina) |
| **Religions:** | Hindu, Buddhist |
| **National Day:** | December 12 |

# NETHERLANDS

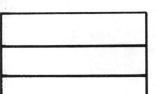

| | |
|---|---|
| **Population:** | 14,864,000 |
| **Capital:** | Amsterdam |
| **Language:** | Dutch |
| **Geography:** | Area: 15,770 Sq. Miles (the size of Massachusetts, Connecticut, and Rhode Island combined) |
| **Religions:** | Roman Catholic, Dutch Reformed |
| **National Days:** | January 31, May 5 |

# NEW ZEALAND

| | |
|---|---|
| **Population:** | 3,397,000 |
| **Capital:** | Wellington |
| **Languages:** | English, Maori |
| **Geography:** | Area: 103,736 Sq. Miles (the size of Colorado) |
| **Religions:** | Anglican, Presbyterian, Roman Catholic |
| **National Days:** | February 6, April 25 |

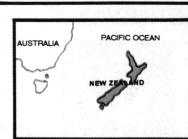

# CARAGUA

| | |
|---|---|
| **Population:** | 3,606,000 |
| **Capital:** | Managua |
| **Languages:** | Spanish, English |
| **Geography:** | Area: 50,193 Sq. Miles (about the size of Iowa) |
| **Religion:** | Roman Catholic |
| **National Days:** | July 19, September 15 |

# IGER

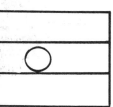

| | |
|---|---|
| **Population:** | 8,154,000 |
| **Capital:** | Niamey |
| **Languages:** | French, Hausa, Djerma |
| **Geography:** | Area: 489,189 Sq. Miles (amost three times the size of California) |
| **Religion:** | Sunni Muslim |
| **National Day:** | December 18 |

# GERIA

| | |
|---|---|
| **Population:** | 118,865,000 |
| **Capital:** | Abuja |
| **Languages:** | English, Hausa, Yoruba, Ibo |
| **Geography:** | Area: 356,667 Sq. Miles (more than twice the size of California) |
| **Religions:** | Muslim, Christian |
| **National Day:** | October 1 |

# ORWAY

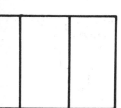

| | |
|---|---|
| **Population:** | 4,214,000 |
| **Capital:** | Oslo |
| **Languages:** | Bokmal, Norwegian (Nynorsk), Lappish, |
| **Geography:** | Area: 125,181 Sq. Miles (slightly larger than New Mexico) |
| **Religion:** | Evangelical Lutheran |
| **National Day:** | May 17 |

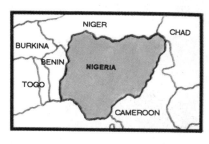

# MAN

| | |
|---|---|
| **Population:** | 1,305,000 |
| **Capital:** | Muscat |
| **Languages:** | Arabic, English, Urdu |
| **Geography:** | Area: 82,030 Sq. Miles (about the size of New Mexico) |
| **Religions:** | Ibadhi Muslim, Sunni Muslim |
| **National Day:** | November 18 |

# KISTAN

| | |
|---|---|
| **Population:** | 117,490,000 |
| **Capital:** | Islamabad |
| **Languages:** | Urdu, Punjabi, provincial lanuages, English |
| **Geography:** | Area: 310,403 Sq. Miles (about the size Texas) |
| **Religion:** | Muslim |
| **National Days:** | March 23, August 14 |

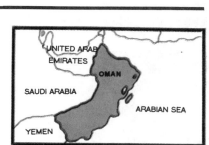

# PANAMA

| | |
|---|---|
| **Population:** | 2,476,000 |
| **Capital:** | Panama City |
| **Languages:** | Spanish, English |
| **Geography:** | Area: 29,208 Sq. Miles (slightly larger than West Virginia) |
| **Religions:** | Roman Catholic, Protestant |
| **National Day:** | November 3 |

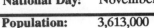

# PAPUA NEW GUINEA

| | |
|---|---|
| **Population:** | 3,613,000 |
| **Capital:** | Port Moresby |
| **Languages:** | English, Melanesian Pidgin, 700 native dialects |
| **Geography:** | Area: 178,260 Sq. Miles (slightly larger than California) |
| **Religions:** | Protestant, Roman Catholic, Lutheran |
| **National Day:** | September 16 |

# PARAGUAY

| | |
|---|---|
| **Population:** | 4,660,000 |
| **Capital:** | Asuncion |
| **Languages:** | Spanish, Guarani |
| **Geography:** | Area: 157,047 Sq. Miles (the size of California) |
| **Religion:** | Roman Catholic |
| **National Day:** | May 14 |

# PERU

| | |
|---|---|
| **Population:** | 22,362,000 |
| **Capital:** | Lima |
| **Languages:** | Spanish, Quechua, Aymara |
| **Geography:** | Area: 496,222 Sq. Miles (three times larger than California) |
| **Religion:** | Roman Catholic |
| **National Day:** | July 28 |

# PHILIPPINES

| | |
|---|---|
| **Population:** | 66,647,000 |
| **Capital:** | Manila |
| **Languages:** | Philipino, English |
| **Geography:** | Area: 115,831 Sq. Miles (slightly larger than Nevada) |
| **Religions:** | Roman Catholic, Protestant, Muslim |
| **National Day:** | June 12 |

# POLAND

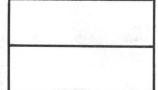

| | |
|---|---|
| **Population:** | 38,363,000 |
| **Capital:** | Warsaw |
| **Language:** | Polish |
| **Geography:** | Area: 120,727 Sq. Miles |
| **Religion:** | Roman Catholic |
| **National Day:** | July 22 |

# ORTUGAL

| | |
|---|---|
| **Population:** | 10,528,000 |
| **Capital:** | Lisbon |
| **Language:** | Portuguese |
| **Geography:** | Area: 36,390 Sq. Miles including the Azores and Madeira Islands (slightly smaller than Indiana) |
| **Religion:** | Roman Catholic |
| **National Day:** | June 10 |

# UERTO RICO

| | |
|---|---|
| **Population:** | 3,336,000 |
| **Capital:** | San Juan |
| **Languages:** | Spanish, English |
| **Geography:** | Area: 3,435 Sq. Miles |

# ATAR

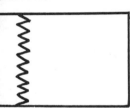

| | |
|---|---|
| **Population:** | 498,000 |
| **Capital:** | Doha |
| **Languages:** | Arabic, English |
| **Geography:** | Area: 4,247 Sq. Miles (smaller than Connecticut and Rhode Island combined) |
| **Religion:** | Muslim |
| **National Day:** | September 3 |

# OMANIA

| | |
|---|---|
| **Population:** | 23,397,000 |
| **Capital:** | Bucharest |
| **Languages:** | Romanian, Hungarian, German |
| **Geography:** | Area: 91,699 Sq. Miles (slightly smaller than New York and Pennsylvania combined) |
| **Religions:** | Romanian, Orthodox, Roman Catholic |
| **National Days:** | May 9, August 23 |

# USSIA

| | |
|---|---|
| **Population:** | 148,041,000 |
| **Capital:** | Moscow |
| **Languages:** | Russian |
| **Geography:** | Area: 6,592,670 Sq. Miles |

# WANDA

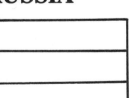

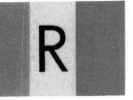

| | |
|---|---|
| **Population:** | 7,603,000 |
| **Capital:** | Kigali |
| **Languages:** | Kinyarwanda, French, Swahili |
| **Geography:** | Area: 10,169 Sq. Miles (the size of Maryland) |
| **Religions:** | Christian, traditional, Muslim, Roman Catholic, Protestant |
| **National Day:** | July 1 |

# SAUDIA ARABIA

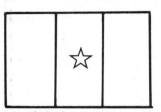

| | |
|---|---|
| **Population:** | 16,758,000 |
| **Capital:** | Riyadh |
| **Language:** | Arabic |
| **Geography:** | Area: 839,996 Sq. Miles (one-third the size of the United States) |
| **Religion:** | Muslim |
| **National Day:** | September 23 |

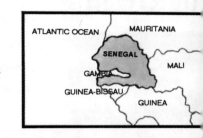

# SENEGAL

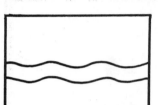

| | |
|---|---|
| **Population:** | 7,740,000 |
| **Capital:** | Dakar |
| **Languages:** | French, tribal languages |
| **Geography:** | Area: 75,750 Sq. Miles (the size of South Dakota) |
| **Religions:** | Muslim, Christian |
| **National Day:** | April 4 |

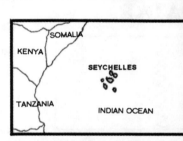

# SEYCHELLES

| | |
|---|---|
| **Population:** | 71,000 |
| **Capital:** | Victoria |
| **Languages:** | English, French, Creole |
| **Geography:** | Area: 171 Sq. Miles |
| **Religion:** | Roman Catholic |
| **National Day:** | June 29 |

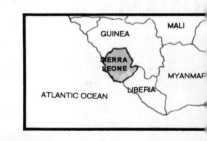

# SIERRA LEONE

| | |
|---|---|
| **Population:** | 4,168,000 |
| **Capital:** | Freetown |
| **Languages:** | English, Mende, Temne |
| **Geography:** | Area: 27,925 Sq. Miles (slightly smaller than South Carolina) |
| **Religions:** | Animist, Muslim, Christian |
| **National Day:** | April 19 |

# SINGAPORE

| | |
|---|---|
| **Population:** | 2,703,000 |
| **Capital:** | Singapore |
| **Languages:** | Chinese, Malay, Tamil, English |
| **Geography:** | Area: 224 Sq. Miles (smaller than New York City) |
| **Religions:** | Buddhist, Taoist, Moslim, Christian |
| **National Day:** | August 9 |

# SLOVENIA

| | |
|---|---|
| **Capital:** | Ljubljana |

# OMALIA

| | |
|---|---|
| **Population:** | 8,415,000 |
| **Capital:** | Mogadishu |
| **Languages:** | Somali, Arabic |
| **Geography:** | Area: 246,300 Sq. Miles (slightly smaller than Texas) |
| **Religion:** | Sunni Muslim |
| **National Day:** | October 21 |

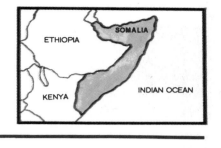

# OUTH AFRICA

| | |
|---|---|
| **Population:** | 39,550,000 |
| **Capital:** | Pretoria Cape Town |
| **Languages:** | English, Afrikaans, Nguni, Tsonga, Sotho and Venda language groups |
| **Geography:** | Area: 472,359 Sq. Miles (about twice the size of Texas) |
| **Religions:** | Christian, Hindu, Muslim |
| **National Day:** | May 31 |

# PAIN

| | |
|---|---|
| **Population:** | 39,623,000 |
| **Capital:** | Madrid |
| **Languages:** | Spanish, Catalan, Galician, Basque |
| **Geography:** | Area: 194,896 Sq. Miles (the size of Arizona and Utah combined) |
| **Religion:** | Roman Catholic |
| **National Days:** | June 24, October 12 |

# RI LANKA

| | |
|---|---|
| **Population:** | 17,135,000 |
| **Capital:** | Colombo |
| **Languages:** | Sinhala, Tamil, English |
| **Geography:** | Area: 25,332 Sq. Miles (about the size of West Virginia) |
| **Religions:** | Buddhist, Hindu, Christian, Muslim |
| **National Day:** | February 14 |

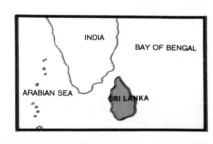

# UDAN

| | |
|---|---|
| **Population:** | 27,220,000 |
| **Capital:** | Khartoum |
| **Languages:** | Arabic, Darfurian, Nilotic languages |
| **Geography:** | Area: 966,757 Sq. Miles (the largest country in Africa, over one-fourth the size of the United States) |
| **Religions:** | Sunni Muslim, Animist, Christian |
| **National Day:** | January 1 |

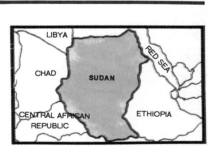

# URINAME

| | |
|---|---|
| **Population:** | 408,000 |
| **Capital:** | Paramaribo |
| **Languages:** | Dutch, Sranan (Creole), Hindu, English |
| **Geography:** | Area: 63,037 Sq. Miles (slightly larger than Georgia) |
| **Religions:** | Muslim, Hindu, Christian |
| **National Day:** | November 25 |

# SWAZILAND

| | |
|---|---|
| **Population:** | 859,000 |
| **Capital:** | Mbabane |
| **Languages:** | English, Si-Swati, Swazi |
| **Geography:** | Area: 6,704 Sq. Miles (slightly smaller than New Jersey) |
| **Religions:** | Christian, indigenous beliefs |
| **National Day:** | September 6 |

# SWEDEN

| | |
|---|---|
| **Population:** | 8,407,000 |
| **Capital:** | Stockholm |
| **Languages:** | Swedish |
| **Geography:** | Area: 173,731 Sq. Miles (larger than California) |
| **Religion:** | Lutheran |
| **National Days:** | June 6, May 30 |

# SWITZERLAND

| | |
|---|---|
| **Population:** | 6,628,000 |
| **Capital:** | Bern |
| **Languages:** | German, French, Italian, Romansch |
| **Geography:** | Area: 15,941 Sq. Miles (as large as Massachusetts, Connecticut, and Rhode Island combined) |
| **Religions:** | Roman Catholic, Protestant |
| **National Day:** | August 1 |

# SYRIA

| | |
|---|---|
| **Population:** | 12,471,000 |
| **Capital:** | Damascus |
| **Languages:** | Arabic, Kurdish, Armenian |
| **Geography:** | Area: 71,498 Sq. Miles (the size of North Dakota) |
| **Religions:** | Sunni Muslim, other Muslim, Christian |
| **National Day:** | April 17 |

# TAIWAN
### (REPUBLIC OF CHINA)

| | |
|---|---|
| **Population:** | 20,454,000 |
| **Capital:** | Taipeh |
| **Languages:** | Mandarin Chinese, Taiwan, Hakka dialects |
| **Geography:** | Area: 13,885 Sq. Miles (about the size of Connecticut and New Hampshire combined) |
| **Religions:** | Buddhism, Taoism, Confucianism |
| **National Day:** | October 10 |

# TAJIKISTAN

| | |
|---|---|
| **Capital:** | Dushanbe |
| **Language:** | Tajik |

# TANZANIA

| | |
|---|---|
| **Population:** | 26,070,000 |
| **Capital:** | Dar-es-Salaam |
| **Languages:** | Kiswahili, Swahili, English |
| **Geography:** | Area: 364,886 Sq. Miles (more than twice the size of California) |
| **Religions:** | Muslim, Christian, traditional beliefs |
| **National Day:** | April 27 |

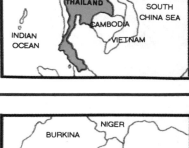

# THAILAND

| | |
|---|---|
| **Population:** | 54,890,000 |
| **Capital:** | Bangkok |
| **Languages:** | Thai, regional dialects |
| **Geography:** | Area: 198,456 Sq. Miles (about the size of Texas) |
| **Religions:** | Buddhist, Muslim |
| **National Day:** | December 5 |

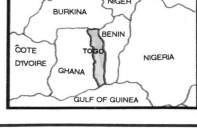

# TOGO

| | |
|---|---|
| **Population:** | 3,566,000 |
| **Capital:** | Lome |
| **Languages:** | French, Ewe, Kabra |
| **Geography:** | Area: 21,622 Sq. Miles (slightly smaller than West Virginia) |
| **Religions:** | traditional, Christian, Muslim |
| **National Day:** | April 27 |

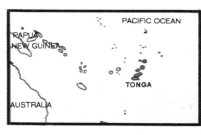

# TONGA

| | |
|---|---|
| **Population:** | 108,000 |
| **Capital:** | Nuku'alofa |
| **Languages:** | Tongan, English |
| **Geography:** | Area: 270 Sq. Miles (smaller than New York City) |
| **Religions:** | Free Wesleyan, Roman Catholics, Free Church of Tonga, Methodist |
| **National Day:** | July 4 |

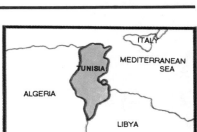

# TUNISIA

| | |
|---|---|
| **Population:** | 8,094,000 |
| **Capital:** | Tunis |
| **Languages:** | Arabic, French |
| **Geography:** | Area: 63,170 Sq. Miles (about the size of Missouri) |
| **Religion:** | Muslim |
| **National Day:** | June 1 |

# TURKEY

| | |
|---|---|
| **Population:** | 58,581,000 |
| **Capital:** | Ankara |
| **Languages:** | Turkish, Kurdish, Arabic |
| **Geography:** | Area: 301,381 Sq. Miles (twice the size of California) |
| **Religions:** | Muslim, Christian, Jewish |
| **National Day:** | October 29 |

# TURKMENISTAN

| | |
|---|---|
| **Population:** | 3,622,000 |
| **Capital:** | Ashkhabad |
| **Language:** | Turkmen |
| **Geography:** | Area: 188,420 Sq. Miles |

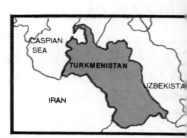

# UGANDA

| | |
|---|---|
| **Population:** | 18,690,000 |
| **Capital:** | Kampala |
| **Languages:** | English, Luganda, Swahili, Bantu and Nilotic languages |
| **Geography:** | Area: 93,354 Sq. Miles (slightly smaller than Oregon) |
| **Religions:** | Christian, Muslim, traditional beliefs |
| **National Day:** | October 9 |

# UKRAINE

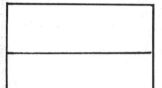

| | |
|---|---|
| **Population:** | 51,839,000 |
| **Capital:** | Kiev |
| **Language:** | Ukrainian |
| **Geography:** | Area: 233,200 Sq. Miles |

# UNITED ARAB EMIRATES

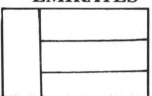

| | |
|---|---|
| **Population:** | 2,250,000 |
| **Capital:** | Abu Dhabi |
| **Languages:** | Arabic, Farsi, English, Hindi, Urdu |
| **Geography:** | Area: 32,000 Sq. Miles (the size of Maine) |
| **Religions:** | Muslim, Christian, Hindu |
| **National Day:** | December 2 |

# UNITED KINGDOM

| | |
|---|---|
| **Population:** | 57,121,000 |
| **Capital:** | London |
| **Languages:** | English, Welsh, Gaelic |
| **Geography:** | Area: 94,226 Sq. Miles (slightly smaller than Oregon) |
| **Religions:** | Church of England, Roman Catholic |
| **National Days:** | April 23, (England), November 30 (Scotland), March 1 (Wales) |

# UNITED STATES OF AMERICA

| | |
|---|---|
| **Population:** | 250,372,000 |
| **Capital:** | Washington D.C. |
| **Languages:** | English, Spanish |
| **Geography:** | Area: 3,618,770 Sq. Miles including 50 states and District of Columbia (world's fourth largest country) |
| **Religions:** | Protestant, Roman Catholic, Jewish |
| **National Day:** | July 4 |

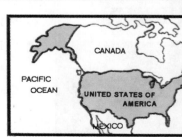

# RUGUAY

| | |
|---|---|
| **Population:** | 3,002,000 |
| **Capital:** | Montevideo |
| **Language:** | Spanish |
| **Geography:** | Area: 68,037 Sq. Miles (the size of Washington State) |
| **Religion:** | Roman Catholic |
| **National Day:** | August 25 |

# ZBEKISTAN

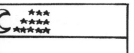

| | |
|---|---|
| **Population:** | 20,322,000 |
| **Capital:** | Tashkent |
| **Geography:** | Area: 172,590 Sq. Miles |

# ANUATU

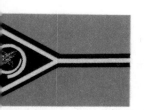

| | |
|---|---|
| **Population:** | 170,000 |
| **Capital:** | Vila |
| **Languages:** | Bislama, English, French |
| **Geography:** | Area: 5,700 Sq. Miles |
| **Religions:** | Presbyterian, Anglican, Roman Catholic, Animist |
| **National Day:** | July 30 |

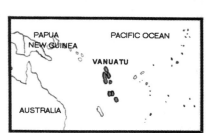

# ATICAN CITY

| | |
|---|---|
| **Population:** | 778 |
| **Capital:** | Vatican City |
| **Languages:** | Italian, Latin |
| **Geography:** | Area: 108.7 acres |
| **Religion:** | Roman Catholic |
| **National Days:** | Christmas, Easter |

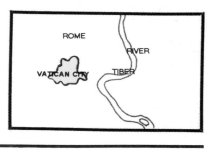

# ENEZUELA

| | |
|---|---|
| **Population:** | 20,189,000 |
| **Capital:** | Caracas |
| **Languages:** | Spanish, Indian languages |
| **Geography:** | Area: 352,143 Sq. Miles (more than twice the size of California) |
| **Religion:** | Roman Catholic |
| **National Days:** | April 19, June 24, July 5, July 24, October 12 |

# IETNAM

| | |
|---|---|
| **Population:** | 68,488,000 |
| **Capital:** | Hanoi |
| **Languages:** | Vietnamese, French, English, Chinese |
| **Geography:** | Area: 128,401 Sq. Miles (the size of New Mexico) |
| **Religions:** | Buddhist, Confucianist, Taoist, Roman Catholic, Animist, Muslim, Protestant |
| **National Day:** | September 2 |

# WESTERN SAMOA

| | |
|---|---|
| **Population:** | 169,000 |
| **Capital:** | Apia |
| **Languages:** | Samoan, English |
| **Geography:** | Area: 1,133 Sq. Miles (the size of Rhode Island) |
| **Religions:** | Protestant, Roman Catholic |
| **National Day:** | January 1 |

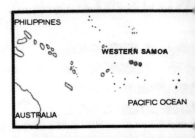

# YEMEN

| | |
|---|---|
| **Population:** | 13,310,000 |
| **Capital:** | Sana |
| **Language:** | Arabic |
| **Geography:** | Area: 205,356 Sq. Miles |
| **Religions:** | Sunni Muslim, Shute Muslim |

# YUGOSLAVIA

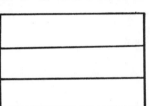

| | |
|---|---|
| **Population:** | 23,864,000 |
| **Capital:** | Belgrade |
| **Languages:** | Serbo-Croatan, Albanian, Hungarian, Macedonian, Slovenian |
| **Geography:** | Area: 98,766 Sq. Miles (the size of Wyoming) |
| **Religions:** | Eastern Orthodox, Roman Catholic, Muslim |
| **National Day:** | November 29 |

# ZAIRE

| | |
|---|---|
| **Population:** | 37,832,000 |
| **Capital:** | Kinshasa |
| **Languages:** | French, Kiswahili, Tshiluba, Kikongo, Lingala |
| **Geography:** | Area: 905,563 Sq. Miles (one-fourth the size of the United States) |
| **Religions:** | Christian, Muslim |
| **National Day:** | November 24 |

# ZAMBIA

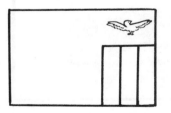

| | |
|---|---|
| **Population:** | 8,119,000 |
| **Capital:** | Lusaka |
| **Languages:** | English, Bemba, Tonga, Malawi, Lozi |
| **Geography:** | Area: 290,586 Sq. Miles (larger than Texas) |
| **Religions:** | Animist, Roman Catholic, Protestant, Hindu, Muslim |
| **National Day:** | October 24 |

# ZIMBABWE

| | |
|---|---|
| **Population:** | 10,205,000 |
| **Capital:** | Harare |
| **Languages:** | English, Shona, Sindebele |
| **Geography:** | Area: 150,803 Sq. Miles (slightly larger than Montana) |
| **Religions:** | traditional tribal beliefs, Christian |
| **National Day:** | April 18 |

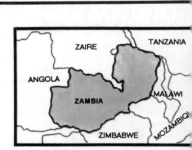